NEW APPRECIATIONS IN
HISTORY 14

The Personal Rule of Charles I 1629-40

by G. E. Aylmer

The Historical Association

59a Kennington Park Road, London SE11 4JH

The portrait of King Charles I (1600-1649) reproduced on the front cover was painted by Daniel Mytems in 1633, eight years after his accession to the throne. Another portrait (in the National Portrait Gallery) of the king standing bareheaded, with his crown and sceptre beside him, was painted by Mytens in 1631.

The picture on the back cover shows a doorway in the King's Manor, York, which was the headquarters of the Council of the North until 1641. Its last Lord President was Thomas Wentworth, created Earl of Strafford in 1640, but executed the following year. He caused his own coat of arms to be placed above this doorway — an act which his enemies were swift to condemn.

Acknowledgements
I am indebted to three younger historians, who have kindly read the text and suggested improvements to it: Anthony Fletcher, John Morrill and Kevin Sharpe. None of them should be held responsible for any remaining errors or misjudgements. I am grateful to my wife for skilful editing and for having taken charge of the illustrations. I also wish to acknowledge the valuable help of Ms Margaret Pierre, the Historial Association's Publications Secretary, and to thank Colleen McMillan for having typed the final version.

Illustrations
The Mytens portrait of Charles I, on the front cover, is reproduced by kind permission of the Trustees of the Rt. Hon. Olive, Countess Fitzwilliam's Chattels Settlement and the Lady Juliet de Chair.

The frontispieces of *Rome for Canterbury* ... (1641), C.13.14 (18) Linc., and of *The Arminian Priests last Petition* (1642), 4 to C.128 Th., are reproduced with the permission of the Bodleian Library.

This reprint has been edited by Pauline Croft

Designed and prepared by Colin Barker, MCSD

ISBN 0 85278 362 0

Originated and published by The Historical Association, 59a Kennington Park Road, London SE11 4JH and printed in Great Britain by The Chameleon Press Limited, 5-25 Burr Road, London SW18 4SG

CONTENTS

The Personal Rule of Charles I 1629-40

Historians are often accused of viewing the past with hindsight, or of being wise after the event. Not being prophets or soothsayers, we have to look backwards in time because we cannot look forwards. The real question is from what vantage point or perspective we view a particular part of the past, and whether we distort its reality by an anachronistic application of ideas or parallels which mislead more than they illuminate. We cannot pretend to ourselves that the subsequent history of England, from the 1640s on, has not happened; we cannot force ourselves to forget about the Civil War, the regicide, the Republic, the Restoration, the Revolution of 1688-9 and so on. Yet we have to guard against misunderstanding what was happening before 1640-42, through seeing the preceding years exclusively from a later standpoint.

A good starting point is to ask ourselves whether there was anything distinctive or unusual about the life of the country and the way in which it was governed under Charles I before the re-call of parliament in 1640. There are some obvious differences between the 1630s and the previous decade. By contrast with the years 1624-9 England was at peace; secondly, after the assassination of George Villiers first Duke of Buckingham in August 1628, there was no single favourite or chief minister who dominated the government and its politics; thirdly, whereas five parliaments met for eight sessions between January 1621 and March 1629, there was no meeting of that body for the next eleven years. We should not, however, leap from these straightforward facts to premature conclusions about what is often labelled the 'Personal Rule' or 'Personal Government' of Charles I. Such a description is at most a convenience, and must not become a hindrance to clear historical understanding.

The Royal Government and the Court

The absence of a dominant chief minister or favourite is the least obvious and most debatable of these features. Charles had never been a mere cipher or puppet in Buckingham's hands. Indeed the policies pursued from his accession in 1625 to the favourite's death were at least as much the King's as Buckingham's, some of them, for example in religion, distinctly more so. None the less George Villiers enjoyed a primacy in the King's affections, in which — unlike Charles's father — there was no homosexual element; and no-one else was ever to have the same primacy in the direction and execution of royal policy. At the age of twenty-nine the King came out of tutelage. For the first three or four years his marriage to the French Catholic princess Henrietta Maria (sister of Louis XIII, who reigned 1610-43) does not seem to have been very happy, but during the 1630s it unquestionably became so, though this may have owed as much to the arrival of children as to the disappearance of Buckingham. The Queen also gradually became more influential politically.

Even so, we should not think of Charles quite as his own 'prime minister'. Although reasonably conscientious and, indeed, keenly interested in some areas of government, especially foreign relations, he did not personally direct affairs from day to day, let alone from hour to hour, as Philip II of Spain had tried to do earlier or as Louis XIV and Frederick the Great were to do later. For instance, during the twenty-six months from 1 May 1629 to 30 June 1631, the king is recorded as having attended 19 out of 198 meetings of the Privy Council, the supreme executive as well as advisory body of government. On the other hand, for a nine-month period of 1637-8 he was present at 25 out of 80 recorded meetings, during which span of time the median attendance of all 28 privy councillors was only 38. These figures exclude council committees, as well as royal meetings with individual ministers; likewise, occasions when councillors went to sign letters but there was no formal meeting. Unfortunately we do not know how often the most important committee, that on Foreign Affairs, met; nor how many times the king presided at it. Nor do we have any regular record of when he saw the Secretaries of State or other individual great officers of state. Charles was active in the diplomatic and some other spheres, but wide areas of government were normally left in his ministers' hands, notably law and finance.

Some of those who held high office were important for long periods but never sought or achieved predominance. Sir Thomas Coventry, Lord Keeper of the Great Seal 1625-40, was perhaps the most respected minister, but never the most powerful. Similarly Henry Montague, first Earl of Manchester, Lord President of the Council then Lord Privy Seal, became less active with advancing years and poor health. Richard Weston, Lord Treasurer 1628-35, created Earl of Portland during that time, was the single most influential figure during the early 1630s. His rivals at the same time found him infuriating, given to evasions and delays if not worse, and he has not had a very good press from historians; but he at least presided over a limited improvement in the Crown's financial position. From 1634 his influence was declining, due to an advancing fatal illness, and accusations of corruption which he failed to rebut, although he was never formally charged. From then until 1638 or 1639 Archbishop William Laud may be said to have occupied a similar position among equals; yet he always had to contend with opponents at the innermost circle of power and royal favour. In 1635-6 Laud was able to prevent the succession to the Treasury of Sir Francis Cottington, who had been Portland's closest ally and lieutenant, as Chancellor of the Exchequer. After twelve months of rivalry between them as Treasury Commissioners, Laud obtained the appointment of his own close friend and one-time Oxford protégé, William Juxon, Bishop of London. There were those who thought that it should have gone instead to Laud's ally Thomas, Viscount Wentworth, who had been in Ireland since 1633, and it may have been the King who missed this chance. Cottington was fobbed off with the Mastership of the Court of Wards and Liveries, the largest independent revenue department after the Exchequer. Cottington, too, irritated Laud and Wentworth, but deserves some credit for his financial achievements. Finally in 1639-40 Wentworth was recalled from Ireland, made Earl of Strafford, and was recognized — fatally for himself — as chief minister, again with some bitter enemies, even among his closest colleagues. Until then he was seldom in London and therefore could not attend council meetings or participate (except by proxy) in court intrigue. Except as judges in the courts of Star Chamber and High Commission neither he nor Laud was directly involved with the judicial part of government. Only during the Treasury Commission of 1635-6 was either of them directly implicated in the régime's financial plans or their execution. Moreover, for much of the time they were only spasmodically consulted on issues of foreign policy. At no time can the Wentworth-Laud partnership be equated with a 'ministry' in the more modern sense. And when they referred to 'Thorough' in their private correspondence this was intended at least as much as a criticism of their colleagues in the King's service as a blue-print for the government of the country. Yet, as will be argued below, without a shift towards absolutism, Charles's system was bound to fail, and more traditional ways were sooner or later bound to return.

Some of those who played a leading political role had come up through the court, serving in the royal Bedchamber or some other branch of the household above stairs (also known as the Chamber). Prominent among these was James Hay, Earl of Carlisle, who was Groom of the Stole and head of the Bedchamber from 1631 to his death in 1636. Thought by some contemporaries to be about to succeed in Buckingham's vacant place as prime favourite, Carlisle was known as the most extravagant man of his time; he never achieved more than the friendship and favour of two successive monarchs and some limited political influence. Philip Herbert, first Earl of Montgomery, who succeeded his elder brother as fourth Earl of Pembroke in 1630, had also begun his career as a personal favourite of King James. The Herbert brothers had at first promoted, then too late resisted, the rise of Villiers, but had eventually come to terms with him. Even without the death of the elder brother, it is unlikely that the Herberts would have exercised real power, as opposed to the patronage that went with headship of the royal household. Even there,

Pembroke and Montgomery were to be challenged by Henry Rich, Earl of Holland, who succeeded Carlisle as Groom of the Stole. Holland had started his career in the Bedchamber of Charles when he was Prince of Wales; latterly he became more of a favourite of the Queen. This may seem strange because he had some leanings towards puritanism; at least, his elder brother, the Earl of Warwick, was one of the leading Puritan peers and part of the country opposition during the 1630s. Here foreign policy is the explanation: to be Puritan was to be anti-catholic, to be anti-catholic also anti-Spanish, and to be realistically anti-Spanish required one to be pro-French. Hence the connection with the Queen. Another Puritan, or Calvinist-inclined member of her circle, during the mid 1630s, was the head of the Percy family, Algernon, tenth Earl of Northumberland who, besides being granted household offices and minor favours, was advanced to be commander-in-chief of the Navy in 1636 and its formal head as Lord Admiral (vacant since Buckingham's death) in 1638, pending James, Duke of York's majority. Of all the peers who became parliamentarians in the Civil War, the King, we are told, felt bitterest about Northumberland. One of the oldest, and in rank most senior, of the royal councillors was the head of the Howard family, Thomas, Earl of Arundel and Surrey, and Earl Marshall of England, who had earlier helped to inspire Charles's interest in modern painting, as a leading connoisseur and patron of the arts. Disappointed by successive kings of his hope to be restored to the dukedom of Norfolk, dormant since 1572, Arundel had been out of favour for much of the 1620s, even at one time in prison. Buckingham's death certainly smoothed his way; but while he was dignified and in the old-fashioned sense aristocratic, Arundel never got to the very top politically, and probably never aspired to do so. Between 1628 and 1632 the number of Scotsmen on the English Privy Council rose from two to seven. This was a cheap and temporarily effective way of strengthening support for royal policies; it is not clear that any of them counted for much politically in England. By 1638-9 there were eight of them, but, more to the point, two of these were figures of note, the King's Scottish cousins: the ambitious, untrustworthy James, Marquis of Hamilton, and the young, agreeable but rather ineffectual James Stuart, Duke of Lennox, both of whom rose through posts in Charles's own Chamber after his accession. All of those mentioned here, except perhaps Lennox, were of some political consequence at various times during the reign. None of them was a true political heavyweight, to be matched with Villiers, Weston, Laud or Wentworth, although Holland turned out to be one of Strafford's most dangerous enemies when disaster struck in 1640-1. This went back to the early 1630s when he had quarrelled with Portland's son; in spite of the derogatory remarks about the Treasurer with which his and Laud's letters are filled, Wentworth allegedly advised the King to have Holland summarily executed: high-handed indeed if true, since no duel had actually taken place and no treason committed.

If we turn from noble courtiers to professional administrators, until 1632 both the Secretaries of State were strong Protestants, and inclined to favour entering into a continental alliance against the Habsburgs. That is precisely what had been tried in the 1620s, apart from the aberration of Charles and Buckingham becoming involved with war against France at the same time as England was at war with Spain (1627-9). There had been little to show for this policy; and perhaps not surprisingly when the post fell vacant, the new Secretary, Francis Windebank, although a friend and client of Laud, joined the pro-Spanish, allegedly crypto-Catholic, Weston-Cottington axis, 'Thorough's' main rival and *bête noire*. Certainly they favoured an alliance with Spain, whereas Wentworth (and probably Laud) were for neutrality. Whether any of the three actually was a secret Catholic at this time remains unproved; what they were to become on their respective deathbeds or, in the case of Cottington and Windebank, in exile, is another matter — and a case where we should beware of hindsight: with Catholic leanings or sympathies is the most that can safely be said. But by 1639-40 widespread suspicion, especially in the case of Windebank, was more important than the truth. The other Secretary, Sir John Coke, who enjoyed an unusual fourteen-year tenure lasting to the beginning of 1640, was a more traditional anti-Spanish Protestant, but counted for less and less at the highest policy-making level, yet was a faithful executant of the King's domestic and Irish policies.

Charles was also served by some able lawyers. William Noy, the Attorney-General from 1631 to 1634, was a critic of the court and its policies in the parliaments of the 1620s, who like Wentworth proved to be a loyal and most effective royal servant, discarding his previous Country outlook. His successor, Sir John Bankes, was equally reliable but less original, also less controversial. Sir John Finch, who replaced Coventry as Lord Keeper at the beginning of 1640, had been Speaker of the House of Commons in 1628-9, when many felt that he had been excessively subservient to the Crown; but he was particularly unpopular because, as Chief Justice, he had lobbied the other judges on the King's behalf about the legality of Ship Money as a levy on the whole country in time of peace. Before this, two senior judges had been removed for being politically unsound, as had happened to the great Sir

Edward Coke back in James's reign. While many prominent common lawyers were politically, or on religious grounds, out of sympathy with the Court, we should not think of the common law as anti-monarchical, or generally opposed to royal policy. Lawyers with political ambitions, like peers and other landowners, had to compete for office and favour. As with diplomats who had served abroad, they were perhaps a little more likely to gain preferment through their professional expertise than was usually the case with those who were primarily courtiers. For example, Sir John Coke's successor as Secretary, Sir Henry Vane* had rather unusually worked his way up through the hierarchy of the Household below stairs; the grounds for his appointment as Secretary were generally reckoned to be the combined influence of the Queen and Hamilton. It was certainly one of the worst choices that Charles could have made.

In the days before a modern civil service and modern political parties, men entered and rose in the King's service through family and personal connections, sometimes through purchasing an office and occasionally by inheriting one. This did not rule out people rising on merit, though it was difficult to get started that way. In the law, the church, finance, diplomacy and medicine, ability was always a factor, and sometimes the decisive one. Court favour and connection, knowing the right person, or knowing someone else who did, was often the only way to get in and get on. As a variant on this, in the parliaments of the 1620s some MPs had made their mark as critics of the Court and of the King's ministers, largely in order to advance their own claims to office. Wentworth, who became a peer and then Lord

* *Usually known as the elder, to distinguish him from his son, Sir Henry Vane the younger, who was Governor of Massachusetts at an early age, and subsequently a leading parliamentarian and then republican.*

President of the North in 1628, is the foremost example of this; Noy is another. When no parliaments were called, the royal court became all the more important as the avenue to office, also to other grants and acts of kingly favour. This explains the great emphasis that some historians have put on court faction in the political process, but there is a danger of misunderstanding here. The King's Bedchamber staff and other household intimates were clearly important in helping aspirants to gain access, effecting introductions and obtaining the royal signature to warrants. On the other hand their political importance, in terms of the other wider issues of the day, both foreign and domestic, was much more limited. This seems to have been more true after the Buckingham era than it had been from James's accession down to 1628. Thus, Charles's Groom of the Stole from 1625 to 1631 was a political nonentity. Even men as close to the King as Endymion Porter and Will Murray were more important as agents and go-betweens than as policy-makers.

Charles was criticised during his own time, and often has been since, for having allowed himself to be excessively influenced by his wife and others, notably in the years leading up to the Civil War. But for most of the time from his accession, certainly from the death of Buckingham until the recall of parliament, he was essentially his own master. He was his own head of government as well as formal head of state. That is not to say that he master-minded all the policies with which his rule is associated, playing off the rival groups and factions within his court and government, in order to keep his options open, or to pursue his own chosen policies while masking them behind these rivalries. This would be to make him much more the master of the situation than he was. Did Charles in fact intend to change the government of the country; was he trying to create something nearer to an absolute monarchy? He had a temperamental passion for order: for harmony and seemliness. Did this amount to a new frame of government?

The Constitution and the Law

In the 1630s, as earlier, there was a wide measure of agreement on how the country should be governed. The King was expected to rule as well as to reign. His powers and prerogatives were very wide indeed, but were to be exercised through the traditional laws and customs of the land, except in time of sudden emergency. This meant that the King was expected to call a parliament, when he wanted new laws enacted, extra taxes voted, or to consult generally with the estates of the realm or their representatives on the country's problems. No doubt under James I, as under earlier monarchs, certainly including Queen Elizabeth about whom there grew up a great deal of myth in the course of the seventeenth century, some parliaments went more smoothly than others. Often this owed more to the skill with which they were managed by the royal ministers and councillors than to substantive issues of great principles. And this in return depended on the unity of purpose among them as well as the extent and firmness of royal backing. If Court and Council were divided, this was likely to be reflected, with damaging effects, in parliament. However the Country, in the sense not so much of a modern political opposition as of non-governmental opinion in general, could likewise be divided: regional, social and economic, and ideological issues could all cut across simple Country versus Court lines of division. In any parliament, a large group of MPs were themselves courtiers or officials, but they did not act together like a government party; others were aspirants to office who might be either for or against the

Court on particular issues; many were what we should call backbenchers, provincials visiting the capital occasionally as spokesmen for, and accountable to, their localities. Again they too might be for or against different royal policies; if taxes were to be levied they would want to know why, and might also want evidence of previous grants having been put to good use.

Nor was faction the same as the tension between Court and Country. As a political and personal factor it could often cut across that division, splitting both of them. The rivalry in Yorkshire and at court between Wentworth and the Savil(l)es of Howley and Pontefract** and the conflict over the Bedchamber patronage between Holland and Pembroke in 1636 are examples of this. To write the political history of England in terms of patronage and faction at court is to confuse the oil which is necessary to lubricate a machine with the fuel which drives it along.

One great political issue was strikingly absent during these years, in fact from 1603 to the 1670s. For much of the fifteenth century, and intermittently in the sixteenth century, the succession to the throne and the question of who was its rightful occupant had been the central issue in English political life. Charles I sometimes worried about the excessive popularity of his sister, Elizabeth of Bohemia — the so-called Winter Queen — and of his eldest nephew, the exiled Elector of the Palatinate, but his right to the Crown was effectively unchallenged. Of course, the new element from the previous century was religion, which had been differently 'settled' under each successive monarch from Henry VIII to Elizabeth

---

** *Sir John, first Baron Savile of Pontefract (1556-1630), and his son and heir Thomas, second Baron, Viscount in the Irish peerage, later first Earl of Sussex (? 1590-1658).*

I. While the Elizabethan Settlement of 1559 (with a few later additions like the 39 Articles) continued in force, it did so under some stress and strain, with opposition from both extremes of Papal Catholic, and separatist Puritan. Religious divisions were in turn bound up with foreign policy, war and diplomacy, national security, and even with the country's commercial interest. Decisions on these matters could put the political system under increased strain, due to the English Crown's financial weakness and its military and administrative limitations. Extraneous 'acts of God', such as plague or other epidemics, harvest failures and trade fluctuations, over which governments had little if any control, could intensify these difficulties. The Elizabethan régime had faced a combination of unfavourable circumstances in the mid-1590s: wartime strains coinciding with acute economic difficulties. James' latter years, around about 1620 saw a similar combination of general economic crisis and a major European war.

Early Years of Charles I

Charles's succession in 1625 came at a time of re-alignment in foreign relations, with the country abandoning neutrality and embarking on war with Spain after a twenty-year period of peace. The first summer of the new reign saw one of the worst plague epidemics since the Black Death. After this, conditions improved somewhat until a run of bad harvests from 1629, and a renewed slump in the overseas market for English woollen cloth, easily the country's largest export, on which some districts were dangerously dependent. None the less, when every excuse has been made, the new King made things much worse than they need have been by his actions during the first four years of his reign. First of all he retained his father's last and greatest favourite, George Villiers,

Duke of Buckingham, as his chief political adviser, arousing jealousy and resentment at all levels, from members of the longer-established noble families right down to the common seamen who blamed the Lord Admiral for failures in wartime naval administration (pay, supplies, etc.). This might not have mattered if the English navy and the land forces which it transported had won a great and glorious victory. There were understandable reasons for the failure of the 1625 expedition against Cadiz, and that of 1627 to aid the French Protestants besieged in La Rochelle by capturing the off-shore island of Rhé as a springboard for the relief of the city itself. In the second, Buckingham commanded personally, showing courage in the field, but little strategic sense. Inevitably both were compared with the Elizabethan sea war against Spain, which was seen in retrospect as having been a good deal more successful than it had been in reality.

Charles's first parliament (of 1625) saw disagreement about money, religion and the management of the war. In the second (of 1626), Buckingham's enemies in the Council and the House of Lords had encouraged the Commons to impeach him — a method of attacking unpopular ministers which he and Charles had permitted, indeed encouraged, during the last two parliaments of James (1621 and 1624). The King stuck by his friend. Following the 1626 parliament, the favourite himself helped in some attempts at governmental reform as well as in the new ways of raising money because parliamentary subsidies had been made conditional on the Duke's removal, and the traditional part of the customs had not been renewed in the normal way at the start of a new reign. Charles's third parliament (1628) was initially more conciliatory but, at the end of a long session, resentment against the favourite again broke out in the Commons. While supervising another expedition which was about to be launched to save La Rochelle, the Duke was assassinated by a disgruntled and unbalanced ex-officer; but the removal, thus dramatically, of what one MP had called 'the grievance of grievances' turned out to intensify ill-feeling. The King felt that the killer had been encouraged by the parliamentary attacks on his friend. Whatever might have happened if Buckingham had lived, the reversal of foreign policy which followed, sensible enough in itself on military and diplomatic grounds, aroused fresh suspicions about the government's religious inclinations. Already, in the earlier reversal of his father's foreign policy of detente with Spain, Charles had made secret promises in his marriage treaty with France about easing the conditions of English Catholics, although he and his father had publicly promised to make no such concessions. So there were clashes in each successive parliament over the conduct of the war, first against Spain then France, the supplies needed for its effective prosecution, and latterly on the extent of the Crown's emergency powers to raise men and money, and maintain law and order in time of war. In 1626-7 the King had seemed to many people to be abusing his prerogatives in levying a very large involuntary loan after he had failed to get a vote on subsidies from parliament. When he accepted the Petition of Right in the summer of 1628, he appeared to agree that he ought not to raise money in this way. Apart from the Crown's 'ordinary' or regular revenue (from the royal estates, wardships and purveyance, the profits of justice, and the customs duties which Charles claimed were his by right, and various minor sources) he was only to raise money through parliamentary enactment of subsidies or other taxes. Likewise he agreed that he should not billet soldiers on ordinary householders, or impose martial law, except under such an acute emergency as a foreign invasion. And people were not to be held in prison without trial in the absence of proper legal cause, as had happened to numerous opponents of the forced loan in 1627-8. In the view of many MPs, merchants and others he was already in breach of the financial part of the Petition even before the next session of his third parliament opened in 1629, because of his insistence on the collection of customs duties which he saw as the Crown's by inheritance or prerogative. This was very much Charles's personal policy, not that of his ministers, even though some of them were more prerogative-minded, less constitutionalist than others. The same had been true with the Forced Loan of 1626-7, which Charles had justified on the grounds of his honour being at stake, to provide help (in men, money and supplies) for his uncle, the King of Denmark, who had intervened in the war on the Protestant side, against Spain and Austria, on the understanding that he would receive support from England.

Religion and the Church

All this was made worse by the shift in the monarch's religious preferences after Charles I succeeded James I. Whereas his father had tried to keep some kind of balance between the different parties in the church, the new King pursued a policy of systematic discrimination in favour of high-churchmen and against Puritans. Whether those whom Charles favoured should be called Arminians, after the leading revisionist theoretician in the Dutch Reformed Church, or anti-Calvinists because their main emphasis was on trying to reduce the theological influence of the great French sixteenth-century reformer, or more accurately anti-Puritans because of their campaign to identify their opponents inside the church with the more extreme 'Separatists' and other radical, sometimes seditious, critics of the Elizabethan Settlement and latterly of the Hampton Court Conference and its outcome, continues to be disputed among historians. But there is no doubt about the change in royal policy under Charles, which in turn intensified other religious suspicions. Attacks on individual 'Arminian' churchmen, some of whom were promoted by the King's personal intervention, had been begun in his first parliament and were resumed in the next two. During the session of January to March 1629, the obsessive anti-Catholic feelings of many MPs focused in particular on the recently appointed Lord Treasurer, Richard Weston, and on the recently promoted Bishop of London, William Laud. Underlying the attacks in Weston's case was his pro-Spanish foreign policy, together with his determined support for the King's right to levy the customs duties which had not been authorised by parliament; in Laud's case it was his alliance with the Arminians and his exalted view of the Church's position and of the King's prerogatives. How seriously either was believed to be a secret Papist is impossible to estimate. Laud certainly shared the King's passion for tidiness and decency in church furnishings and the conduct of services; he tended to confuse uniformity with unity, and his personality had a brusqueness which often made his policies appear more extreme than they were.

Why were Puritans and others able to convince themselves that Laud and the Arminians were secret Catholics, agents of Rome, and the King either their unwitting dupe or — even worse — their fellow-travelling ally? First, the alterations in the form of worship, the lay-out and fittings of churches, and generally in the outward observances of religion, seemed to point back to pre-Reformation times; secondly, the role of the clergy was

These woodcuts from **The Arminian Priests
last Petition**, *1642*, and **Rome for
Canterbury ... Life of William Laud**, *1641*,
show the hatred felt for the Arminians as
crypto-Papists, and the way in which their

Rome for Canterbury:

Or a true Relation of the Birth, and Life, of *William Laud*, Arch-bifhop of *Canterbury*:

Together with the whole manner of his proceeding, both in the *s*tar-Chamber, High-commiffion *Court*, in his owne Houfe, and fome obfervations of him in the Tower.

With his carriage at the fight of the Deputyes going to the place of Execution, &c.

Dedicated to all the Arminian Tribe, or *Ganterburian* Faction, in tho yeare of grace, 1641.

Whereunto is added all the Articles by which he ftands charged of High Treafon. &c.

Printed alfo in the fame. 1641.

unpopularity was used as a propaganda
weapon against William Laud and the
bishops. The theme is very similar to the
twentieth century concept of a 'fifth column',
first used in the Spanish Civil War (1936-9).

being magnified, and the sacraments exalted above preaching; thirdly, in order to improve the wealth as well as status of the clergy, efforts were made to recover tithes and church livings from lay hands and even to restore other one-time church property; fourthly, there was a move away from the predominance of Calvinist theological ideas, especially the doctrine of double predestination (of some to eternal salvation, of others to perpetual damnation) which had characterised the English church for the previous two generations; finally, accompanying this, Calvinists were being typecast as Puritans, and so in turn as separatists and subversives. Conversely, Puritan resistance made the King, Laud and their supporters less flexible and accommodating than they would probably otherwise have been.

The Calvinist-inclined Archbishop of Canterbury, George Abbott (appointed by James back in 1611), was suspended from all but priestly functions in 1627-8 for refusing to allow publication of an Arminian sermon exalting the royal prerogative. For the rest of his life he was largely inactive as metropolitan, and in politics. On his death in 1633 Laud was promoted to succeed him; indeed the King may have promised Laud the archbishopric as early as 1625 or 1626. Meanwhile in the northern province two Laudian or Arminian-inclined Archbishops (1628-29 and 1629-31) were followed by a third, Richard Neile, who had actually helped to advance Laud's own career in the 1600s, and was unquestionably anti-Calvinist and anti-Puritan in his own right. Not all the diocesan bishops were adherents of Laud and Neile, supporters of the King's ecclesiastical preferences, even in the mid- and later 1630s; but at least one, Matthew Wren (at Norwich 1635-38 and Ely 1638-42), was more extreme than either archbishop. Others were still Calvinists or dated from the Jacobean balance of forces. The increasing extent of the high-church party's victory was one factor in emigration to New England; at the same time it drove some individuals into exile in the Netherlands, or into secret opposition at home. So there was a vicious circle: Laud and the Puritans each seemed worse, in the sense of being more extreme, to the other than they actually were. In his attitude to Rome, it is true that Laud hoped for the eventual re-union of all churches — Catholic, Protestant and Orthodox — rather than for the total overthrow and destruction of the Papacy as the embodiment of Antichrist, as many militant Protestants, not only extreme Puritans, still did; but James I too wanted re-union. Then as now, the question was, on whose terms was it to be? For a truly ecumenical solution to be feasible, a great change in outlook would be necessary on the part of Catholics as well as Protestants.

The Absence of Parliament

That Charles I was able to rule for so long without calling another parliament, with a tolerable measure of success and with relatively little open opposition, may therefore seem surprising. The so-called 'halcyon years' down to 1637 were possible first and foremost because the country was at peace. Coincidentally with this, after years of real hardship, economic conditions improved from 1631 on. Harvests were better, and the country's foreign trade and merchant shipping benefitted from the policy of neutrality and retrenchment. Politically, the government's critics in the House of Commons had seriously over-reached themselves in the 1629 session. The manner of its ending, with the King's emissary denied entry to the chamber while the Speaker was forcibly held down in his chair, so that three provocative resolutions could be read and carried, enabled Charles to portray himself as the injured party. Parliament was seen by others, too, as having allowed itself to be manipulated by a small, unscrupulous and factious minority in one House. The King's proclamations which followed, the first justifying the dissolution, the second banning rumours of a new parliament until he should judge the time fit to call one, exploited this situation successfully. Certainly, the three resolutions, against the payment and collection of the customs duties and against Arminianism, had no legal force or constitutional standing. The majority in the House of Lords had gone along with the Commons on the Petition of Right in 1628, but they had no part in this débacle. Particular aspects of royal policy were undoubtedly disliked by specific interest groups; but it was only when circumstances again changed adversely for the Crown that the suspicions and resentments of 1625-29 once more became an effective source of opposition.

Revenue and Expenditure

Some historians have seen a logical progression in Charles I's financial policies from the earliest years of his reign. Having failed to obtain a vote of more than a very few subsidies from his first parliament, and none from his second, the King had then immediately proposed to raise money by a 'benevolence', or theoretically voluntary capital levy, a practice which had actually been illegal since the later fifteenth century. When this looked like running into serious resistance, he at once resorted instead to the 'Forced Loan', again voluntary in theory, easily the largest of its kind ever known, which yielded the equivalent of several subsidies. After the cessation of parliaments in 1629, his next extraordinary measure for raising money illustrated his government's passion for antiquarian research. An ancient practice was revived to the effect that all landowners worth over £40 a year should turn up to be knighted at a new King's coronation. And all those who had failed to do so in 1626 were then fined on a graded scale, according to their estimated income from their estates. This yielded the equivalent of rather over two parliamentary subsidies, of which the King's third parliament in 1628 had voted five, as a *quid pro quo* for the Petition of Right and on the assumption that the war was going to be continued. Next came the enforcement of ancient laws about the boundaries of royal forests; over a period of years swingeing fines were imposed on private landowners, including some of the wealthiest peers and gentry, who had allegedly encroached on the historic limits of these forests. Commissions to investigate the wrongful enclosure of open fields and common lands were vexatious to the landowners in those counties which were reviewed for this purpose. But this brought in little money. Nor did the long-lasting commission to investigate the taking of excessive fees by royal officials and the existence of innovated (that is, wrongly established) offices, which merely compounded with a few of the most notorious offenders. Potentially more serious, a way was found of getting around the act passed in James's last parliament against monopolies, without openly breaking the law. Some of these grants to companies or corporations were merely minor irritants, but by the later 1630s they had been instituted on the near necessities of soap and salt; and so, through the monopolists' payments to the Crown, were set fair to become a disguised form of indirect taxation. Meanwhile the yield from the ancient prerogative of royal wardship was raised to an unprecedented level, partly because middle-men and 'brokers' got less, partly because the burden on the estates of families in wardship, with under age or female heirs, was made heavier. The second most considerable feudal revenue, from Purveyance and Cartage (the cost of providing the royal household at below market prices, with supplies of food, drink, fuel, lighting and transport), was maintained but not significantly increased. The burden of Cartage increased with the transportation of more timber for shipbuilding.

The yield from the different branches of the customs duties on exports and imports made up easily the largest single element in the Crown's ordinary or regular revenues. So its success in defeating the boycott and nonpayment campaigns which had been attempted by some London merchants (in 1628-30) was a significant victory. Not only did the government continue to levy the traditional Tunnage and Poundage duties, which should have been granted to Charles for life in 1625, but had instead only been offered him for one year, a proposal which he had spurned then, and when it was repeated in 1626. In addition, the so-called Impositions, or additional duties levied mainly on new kinds of imports, first introduced in the 1600s but never validated by parliament, were successfully collected, together with the more recent additions to them, the 'new Impositions'; and finally, from the mid and later 1630s a further levy of new 'New Impositions', on top of all these, bringing the total raised from the customs far above anything achieved before. The revenue from Crown lands, the personal estates of the monarch and other members of the royal family were appreciably improved, but not to any sensational extent. As a landlord, the King was also a patron; his relationship with his own tenants was not merely a commercial one.

Setting aside new taxes or extraordinary sources of revenue, this meant that by the mid-1630s the Crown's income was at last outstripping inflation and growing in real terms. The crown jewels were redeemed from the hands of international pawnbrokers; the King steadily enlarged his splendid art collection. At the same time some limited economies were imposed on the main spending departments: the Navy, the Ordnance Office, forts, castles and garrisons, the royal Household itself. The last of these was the most resistant to genuine reductions, as against accounting devices designed to preserve the vested interests of officials. As on the administrative and judicial sides of government, so in finance, little or nothing was achieved by way of structural reform or qualitative change. It was almost entirely a matter of doing the same old things slightly better than they had been done in the past, or at least for a long time. Whereas in the 1620s the Crown had had to resort to further land sales, involving the liquidation of capital assets, in order to pay its debts and secure its credit, by the mid-1630s there was a modest and growing surplus on current account, and royal credit seemed, on the surface at least, to have been restored to a more buoyant state.

By common consent at the time, and among subsequent historians, the greatest single novelty in financial policy was the institution of Ship Money as a regular peacetime levy. The historic precedents for this were all from times of war. The King and the Council justified the initial demand, for ships or the monetary equivalent, in 1634 (to be brought in by 1635), through the immediate threat to the country from the rapidly growing naval strength of both the French and the Dutch, as well as the depredations of North African pirates around the English coasts. Again in line with precedent, this was levied only from seaports and seaboard counties. Then, in 1635, the tax was extended to the whole of England and Wales. Ship

Money was levied at a rate equivalent to over four parliamentary subsidies a year in 1636, 1637 and 1638; it was then cut to the level of more like one and a half subsidies for 1639, and was intended to be increased again to the 1636-38 level for 1640. The official records, in the privy council registers and the state papers, are full of complaints about non- payment, or at least of delays and excuses from those responsible for its collection, and pleas for reduction of the amounts to be raised. This may be a case where some original records taken in isolation from others, give a misleading impression; until 1639-40 a remarkably high proportion of the scheduled totals was actually paid in. Moreover, whatever the constitutional rights and wrongs of it, the money really was spent, again until near the end, on building, arming and equipping new warships or renovating and refurbishing older ones. We shall return to Ship Money in assessing the extent of opposition to Charles's government before 1640.

Simply considered as a tax it was a good deal more efficient than the traditional parliamentary subsidy, or the even more ancient tenth and fifteenth. The King and the Council decided, on whose recommendation we do not know, not to levy it at a rate of so much in the Pound, but to require each county, and in some cases each city and borough within counties, to raise a fixed quota, set either in ship tonnage or the cash equivalent. When Ship Money was extended to the whole country in 1635-36, these figures were tabulated for the Council, enabling us to see what it was thought that each county could be expected to produce. The relevant individual figure was sent to the Sheriff, or the equivalent official in those towns which were separately assessed. It was then his responsibility to work out how to raise the required amount, by setting a rate in the pound or

otherwise. Granted the sheer inability of any government in early- modern times, indeed until the end of the eighteenth century, to assess the true income of individuals and to tax them on that basis, the county quota was an effective system. And, in spite of the condemnation and banning of Ship Money by parliament in 1640-41, the Long Parliament and succeeding régimes continued to use fixed quotas in direct taxation continuously from 1643 to 1660.

Paradoxically, Charles I's very success in matters of finance — due to a combination of good luck, some efficient ministers and other royal servants, and a few genuinely constructive innovations — was to help cause his downfall. His revenue surplus in 1638 was deceptive, as was his apparent creditworthiness. Both rested on too fragile a basis; and neither was able to withstand the renewed pressures of the following two years.

Foreign Relations

For most of the 1630s the King's main concern was to see whether he could secure the restoration of his brother-in-law (and then his nephew) to the Rhineland Palatinate without re-entering the continental war. Charles's sister, Elizabeth of Bohemia as she was usually known, and her husband Frederick, the leader of the German Calvinists, had been refugees in the Netherlands since the early 1620s. Not only had Frederick failed catastrophically to make good his bid for the Bohemian crown; the cause of Czech independence had gone down with him — as it turned out for just on 300 years. But he had also lost his own dynastic territories in central and west Germany, the Upper and Lower Palatinates respectively, together with his position as one of the seven Electors for the imperial crown of the German Empire. His death, and the succession of his eldest son, Charles Louis, might have made a conditional restoration easier, with less loss of face on both sides. But the exiled Elector's uncle, Charles I, like his father James before him, over-estimated what British neutrality was worth to the European powers, in particular to Spain and Austria. He pursued a tortuous, at times contradictory, and in relation to the Dutch, even dishonest, series of diplomatic campaigns, but at the end of the decade the Palatine royal family were still refugees. This was not all. Charles's earlier unsuccessful intervention in the Buckingham era, followed by his apparently inglorious and fruitless neutrality, contrasted dramatically with the victorious campaigns of the Swedish King, Gustav Adolf, the 'lion of the North' or the Protestant hero, as he later came to be known. The series of Gustavian victories was only ended by the King's death in battle; some even believed that his ultimate aim was to dispossess the Habsburgs and have himself elected and crowned Emperor. In fact the Habsburg-Catholic cause achieved something of a recovery in the 1630s. Without its king as commander-in-chief, the Swedish army proved as defeatable as any other; most of the Lutheran princes in Germany came to terms with the Emperor; only the open entry of France into the war against Spain and Austria prevented an outright Habsburg victory, and ensured that the war dragged on inconclusively for more than another ten years. In 1639 English self-esteem and international prestige suffered another severe setback, when a large Spanish fleet, carrying supplies and re-inforcements for their army in the southern Netherlands, decided to shelter from bad weather off the coast of Kent. With great skill and daring, the Dutch fleet attacked them, inflicting heavy losses and driving other Spanish ships aground on the coast and the reefs to the east of it. Whether or not the battle was technically fought inside or outside English territorial waters, the King had given an assurance of safety to the Spaniards which he was utterly unable to honour.

At times during these years Charles seems to have been genuinely undecided about the best policy to pursue, certainly about the best way to get what he wanted. While he failed to obtain the restoration of his nephew, the country gained considerably from the policy of neutrality, or at any rate of peace and non-intervention. There was a strong case to be made that both France and the Netherlands were potentially more serious rivals, greater threats to the country's vital interests than the already decaying Spanish empire, which was to lose Portugal and the Portuguese overseas possessions in 1640, while at the same time there was to be a temporarily successful revolt in the wealthy province of Catalonia. So Charles's diplomatic failures harmed his prestige and reputation, but in the longer run they perhaps served the country's interests rather well. The Ship Money fleet was not used against the Dutch or the French, though an apologist for Charles might argue that it acted as a successful deterrent and strengthened his diplomatic bargaining position. A single summer cruise each year by ships of the line did virtually nothing to protect English merchant shipping and even places on the south-western coasts from the depredations of North African pirates, who ran a profitable line in plunder and ransom. Nor did it prevent the Dutch herring fleet from coming close inshore along the east coast of England and getting the better of the English fishing boats. As so often, internal and external policies interlocked and interacted on each other.

Tyranny?

One best-selling nineteenth-century radical historian coined the phrase 'the

Eleven Years Tyranny' to describe the Personal Rule. How tyrannical was it? A cynical reply might be that, if J.R. Green had lived in the twentieth century, he would have known the real meaning of tyranny and would not conceivably have used it of Charles's régime. However, a more systematic answer than that seems to be called for. For the most part the King and his ministers kept well within the law. Those MPs who were held to have conspired to disrupt the final sitting of parliament in 1629 were proceeded against in the Court of King's Bench, their conduct not being allowed to be covered by parliamentary privilege. Those who submitted and begged the King's pardon were not in fact brought to trial; three were imprisoned for contumacious refusal to submit, and of these one — the leader of the alleged conspiracy and certainly the moving spirit behind the three resolutions — Sir John Eliot — contracted tuberculosis and died in the Tower (1632), though it is of course possible that the disease would have killed him equally soon even if he had been sent home to Cornwall. His death excited little attention. The other two were still in prison, though not under close confinement, in 1640. The merchants who had tried to avoid paying the customs duties, which they claimed to be illegal, were brought to heel in a similar way, largely through the Court of Exchequer; only one ended up in prison for any length of time. A schoolmaster was sentenced to lose his ears, be flogged, imprisoned and fined, for having toasted Buckingham's assassin during a drinking session in an Oxford college buttery. However, he expressed sufficient repentance to be released and pardoned after two years. Potentially more serious because it involved members of the peerage, a row blew up over the clandestine circulation of a satirical memorandum, setting out the steps which the King should take in order to make himself absolute. A Star Chamber case was

launched, but in the end commonsense prevailed and the proceedings were dropped. A Scottish Puritan pamphleteer was tried and convicted for seditious libel, having made a lengthy and verbally violent attack on the bishops, indeed on the whole institution of episcopacy; he suffered brutal mutilation and indefinite imprisonment. Curiously, the Court of Star Chamber where he was tried, could not inflict the death penalty, although it could order savage corporal punishment short of that. The great majority of Star Chamber cases were private actions brought by people who found it quicker and cheaper than litigation in the traditional common law courts. It is not always easy to see why certain politically sensitive cases were brought there, and others in King's Bench.

A few years later the well-known Puritan lawyer, William Prynne, who had published an immensely long and intemperate attack on the theatre and stage plays, was convicted of libelling the Queen who had recently taken part in amateur theatricals at court. This was by no means the first Puritan attack on the stage: the dramatists, including Shakespeare himself but above all Ben Jonson, had given at least as good as they had got. Nor, as we shall see, was this a simple collision: not all Puritans were against all plays, not all dramatists were supporters of the Court or the high-church party. At any rate Prynne lost his ears (or part of them) and was fined and imprisoned. Then three years later, in 1637, came the most notorious Star chamber case of the whole decade. It was brought again against Prynne, who had managed to go on writing and to get items published in spite of imprisonment, together with Henry Burton, a clergyman who had once been chaplain to Charles as Prince of Wales, and John Bastwick, a medical doctor, for publishing a series of anonymous pamphlets libelling individual bishops and attacking episcopacy. Some of those held responsible for printing and distributing their works were also tried and punished, including a young man who, unlike Prynne, was to become famous in the 1640s, as a genuine hero of popular freedom — John Lilburne. But attention was focused on the representatives of the three great learned professions. The most unattractive feature of this trial was that the two archbishops and the other two bishops, who were among the injured parties in the actions being brought, as privy councillors were automatically judges in Star Chamber; although they abstained from passing sentence, they were later alleged to have watched through a window when the first and most savage part of the penalties were being inflicted. Prynne had his ears cut for the second time, the other two for the first; all were pilloried, flogged and then imprisoned.

More or less concurrently with this John Hampden, a Buckinghamshire landowner and ex-MP, was being sued through the Court of Exchequer for refusing to pay his contribution towards his county's ship money quota. Eventually, in 1638 the case was heard on appeal before all twelve common law judges in what was known as the Court of Exchequer Chamber. Whereas earlier the other eleven judges had all agreed with Chief Justice Finch about the legality of ship money and its coming within the scope of the King's prerogative even in time of peace, now the Crown's case was upheld only by seven to five: a hollow victory indeed, even if only two of the five (Justices Croke and Hutton) found for the defence on substantive rather than narrowly technical grounds. The speeches made on both sides (one of Hampden's counsel was a future royalist, the other, Oliver St John, was to become a leading parliamentarian), and by some from the judges in giving their verdicts, were of the greatest interest. Even St John did not deny the Crown's emergency powers, but instead pleaded a demurrer, arguing that it was not during an emergency that his client had refused to pay; at least one of the judges (Berkeley) seemed to argue for a royal prerogative without any limits at all. So Hampden lost his case, but he was never imprisoned; moreover, two peers who had also refused to pay and had incited others to do likewise were not proceeded against. They would have had to be tried by a specially empanelled court of other peers. The King and his advisers judged, no doubt sensibly, that they were more likely to get a clear-cut verdict in their favour against a commoner in the ordinary courts.

There was one other case of some celebrity, or should one say notoriety. Laud's most dangerous political and ecclesiastical rival from the 1620s, John Williams, Dean of Westminster and then Bishop of Lincoln, who had been Lord Keeper of the Great Seal between Bacon and Coventry (1621-5), was charged with having tried to pervert the course of justice. This went back to the time when he had been a councillor in the 1620s; whether or not Williams was guilty of improper behaviour seemed to many people less important than the fact of Laud waging a kind of vendetta against him, and securing a conviction several years after the alleged happenings. At any rate Williams was eventually found guilty, suspended from his episcopal functions and imprisoned (though not very closely) from 1637 to 1640. If his offence was more than a technical one, it is extraordinary that the King should have raised him to the Archbishopric of York in 1641 after the death of Neile, when Parliament had secured his release from prison and restoration to the see of Lincoln and to his seat in the House of Lords. Considering the King's high view of the Church and of episcopacy, it would seem too cynical simply to say that times had changed by then, though indeed they had.

There was no single execution for treason or related offences from 1629 to the spring of 1640, and only a handful even if we include Catholic priests. And the total number of what we would call political prisoners, or prisoners of conscience, was only just into double figures. In the absence of a professional police force, a peacetime standing army, or an effective civil bureaucracy at the local level, the means scarcely existed even if the King had wanted to rule as a tyrant. That he and his government bent the law, misused legal precedent, and acted unwisely, sometimes with excessive severity, is clear enough — and surely beyond dispute. But that is far from adding up to tyranny.

One of the King's main strengths was his ability to use the existing legal system for the enforcement of his policies. Another was the support which he enjoyed from a sufficient majority among the upper classes (peers, gentry and urban élites) for the implementation of his policies at the local level. It was the erosion of this support, largely in the face of fresh demands for money and manpower during 1639-40, together with the crumbling of his financial position, which compelled resort once more to a parliament in the spring of 1640. Until then, such opposition as there was lacked any kind of nationwide forum or focus. There were no newspapers, only handwritten and clandestinely-circulated newsletters. Even sermons could be risky outside private chapels. Country landowners were meant to live on their estates and not in London, unless they had legal or other *bona fide* business in the capital. Hence the importance ascribed by historians to the board meetings of the Providence Island Company, ostensibly a colonial venture in the West Indies, of which Holland's brother, the Earl of Warwick, was the head and John Pym

— a leading anti-Arminian from the parliaments of the 1620s but also until 1638 a middle-rank revenue official — the Treasurer. Hence too the real or supposed significance of country house visiting, such as the famous meetings — undocumented outside family tradition — which are said to have taken place in the turret room at Broughton Castle, the seat of Viscount Saye and Sele, another key figure in the forces of opposition. The extent of discontent, let alone the prospect of its erupting in any general campaign of resistance to the King's policies, is impossible to assess before the end of the decade. Historians remain sharply divided as to how far, if at all, it is possible to argue back from the 1640s. That all the opposition sprang up suddenly then without any previous growth of discontent is (to the present author) incredible.

Culture and the Arts

In spite of what has been said about Prynne, not all the plays written and staged in these years were pro-court or anti-Puritan. Except for private productions, most theatres may have had socially mixed audiences, with some being weighted more towards an aristocratic or courtly, others more towards a business or mercantile middle-class, clientèle. Middleton in the 1610s and 1620s, and Massinger, who continued to write through the 1630s, are examples of dramatists who were at times nearer to the Country, in an ideological sense, than they were to the Court. Nor were all the lyric, pastoral and love poets 'Cavaliers' in a political sense. The greatest of the 'metaphysicals', as they have come to be called in modern times, Donne and Herbert, passed from the scene in the early 1630s. George Herbert is particularly interesting, in that his religious position could not be called Puritan, possibly not even Calvinist, yet he seems to have been gloomy about the future of true religion in England;

as we have seen, his relatives, the Earls of Pembroke and Montgomery, occupied a somewhat ambivalent political position — in the government and the royal household, yet not wholly of it. Furthermore, some of the poets and playwrights who do seem to have written from a basically pro-court standpoint, felt able to criticise individuals and policies, for human failings and inconsistencies. This is true of Ben Jonson in his last phase as a dramatist; a similar case has recently been argued convincingly in relation to his successors — Davenant, Carew and Townshend. Masques, which were extremely expensive to produce, were the characteristic art form of the royal court and occasionally of other noble households, as with Milton's *Comus* written and put on for the family of Lord Bridgwater, the President of the Council in the Marches of Wales. But it certainly does not follow that Davenant and the other script writers for the masques were sycophantic hacks, incapable of raising a critical note. Much here is bound to depend on the taste and judgment of the individual historian: I would want to suggest that the finest pieces written during these years were the early poems of Milton, where we can see his religious commitment beginning to show through in *Lycidas*, and the lyrics of Robert Herrick, who lived in a remote country parsonage but was unquestionably a strong Anglican and royalist. Despite the brilliant essay of that name by Dame Veronica Wedgwood in her volume *Velvet Studies*, it is doubtful whether the 'Cavalier Poets' existed as a coherent group. George Wither and Edmund Waller, besides Milton, were future parliamentarians.

Did the arts enjoy a 'golden age' before the dull night of puritanism set in? Rubens' ceilings in the Banqueting House in Whitehall, Inigo Jones's neo-Palladian masterpiece, the Queen's House at Greenwich, the best of Vandyck's portraits, would have been adornments to any age. In the intellectual life of the time, Thomas Hobbes was tutor and companion to the Cavendish family at Chatsworth, but he had, so far, written relatively little, and none of his most famous books was published before the 1640s; William Harvey, physician to the King, had already made his fundamental discovery of the circulation of the blood; a provincial doctor, Sir Thomas Browne of Norwich, was writing some of the works for which he is remembered; an Oxford don, Robert Burton of Christ Church, was producing the final revised edition of his encyclopaedic *Anatomy of Melancholy*; the young Lord Falkland's circle at his country house in Great Tew, north of Oxford, included many of the finest intellects of the time, and has been seen as a kind of link between the Erasmian Christian humanists of the early sixteenth century and the moderate (i.e. non-revolutionary) Enlightenment of the eighteenth, though this is probably to make intellectual pedigrees too like genealogical ones, to trace the descent of ideas over-literally. How the arts, science and thought would have developed without the cataclysmic events of the 1640s is a 'might-have-been' question to which no answer is possible. We can only say that in spite of ideological divisions and party conflicts, gross inequalities in wealth and status, and the operation of a censorship over printed publications, this was a society where the life of the mind and spirit was far from being dulled or stilled.

The population of England and Wales had grown from about four millions in 1600 to just over five by 1640, that is approximately one person for every nine today. Many more of the 'top people' still knew each other personally. The twin cities of London and Westminster constituted not only a political and economic capital, but a cultural matrix too; for all that, there was a fashion for pastoral in verse and a widespread pretence of preferring not so much Country to Court politically, as *rus* to *urbs* as a way of life. Fashion indeed transcended political, even religious, divisions. Country or opposition peers, as well as the royal family and their circle, wanted themselves to be painted by Vandyck. Taste in dress, architecture and interior decoration, too, cut across such divisions. A few art forms or tastes were specific to one party, anathema to the other. These included sixteenth-century Italian paintings with nude figures or other sexually explicit themes, painted glass and carving in churches with representations of the deity, angels or saints, church music to accompany choral and organ-led services, over-stimulating erotic verse. None of these were acceptable to the Puritan-inclined sections of society; all were prominent features in the court circle of Charles and Henrietta Maria. So, while culture was not polarised between sensual hedonists and repressive killjoys, there were differences of emphasis, a celebration of contrasting virtues and caution against distinct vices.

Much of this might seem to apply only to the literate and those at least moderately well off. Perhaps there were what some historians would call distinctive 'high' and 'low' cultures; but again we should probably not think of English life as polarised between élite and popular, any more than between courtly and Puritan. As in any society, there were differences in intelligence, sensitivity and cultivation, likewise differences of opportunity. So it is possible to identify élite and popular sports, pastimes and art forms but with a considerable overlap, as in the theatre audiences or various country pursuits. Gradations of wealth and status were also reflected in social and family life. The upper classes tended to marry younger, to have larger families

(possibly because fewer of the mothers breast-fed their babies), and to live longer. In almost all of this the England of Charles I was little different from the preceding and following periods, or from other pre-industrial countries in early-modern times. The English and Welsh were, however, almost uniquely fortunate in not having been invaded for a very long time, and in not having had a nation-wide civil war, as opposed to regional revolts, for a century and a half.

The British Problem

The Crown's renewed difficulties from 1638 on were very largely of the King's own making. Two fundamental changes in British history, both dating from 1603, underlay this: the union of the crowns of Scotland and England with the accession of James VI as James I, and the final English conquest of Ireland, leading to the colonization of Ulster. The full incorporation of Wales under Henry VIII in the 1530s and 1540s had, if anything, strengthened the Tudor dynasty, themselves of partly-Welsh origin. By contrast, the unification of the British Isles which was achieved in 1603 led to new problems. Both Scotland and Ireland were to be the scene of violent upheavals within the space of a few years.

Scotland

Why did the much less wealthy and populous northern kingdom, from which the Stuarts had themselves originated, prove the initial cause of Charles's undoing? Like his father, he ruled Scotland at a distance, by proxy through councillors and ministers sitting in Edinburgh, and by orders sent from London. His only visit, in 1633, was far from a success. There was already suspicion which his presence did nothing to dispel. Ex-church lands which had been in lay

25

hands since the Reformation were thought to be at risk, but aristocratic critics were silenced and, on the surface, calm continued. A new prayer book was drafted by a small group of bishops and other high-churchmen. The King's decision to have this introduced throughout Scotland brought opposition out into the open. There were disorders at the first attempt to use the new service book in July 1637. It was temporarily withdrawn, but the King utterly refused to give way. Once more Archbishop Laud, as primate of all England, was blamed for a policy which was less his than the King's; none the less Laud does seem to have been ill-informed about religious feeling in Scotland, while his ally Wentworth saw the resistance as little more than the product of noble faction led by an oligarchic clique. The most strongly Presbyterian sections of the nobility, the gentry (called lairds in Scotland) and the clergy organized a nation-wide campaign of subscription to the document known as the National Covenant, in which people pledged themselves to uphold the existing church system and forms of worship. Support for the Covenant was by no means unanimous; no doubt there was a good deal of coercion, or subscription merely out of apathy, to avoid trouble. In Aberdeenshire, and parts of the far north west, Catholic and Episcopalian members of the nobility led more general refusals to subscribe. None the less, support for the Covenant was a formidable movement, and came to be coupled with demands for recall of the Scottish parliament and for a meeting of the General Assembly of the Church, both of which the Covenanters clearly expected to control; and it soon became clear that, if necessary, they would not stop short of armed, physical resistance.

The King seems to have decided to coerce the Scots, or rather the Covenanter element among them, by August 1638. On the one hand he was misled by what Juxon and Cottington told him about his financial position; there was indeed a modest reserve in hand, but it was quite inadequate for what the King now had in mind. On the other hand, Charles was, throughout, advised by a very small group of councillors, who had either lost touch with their own Scottish background (such as Lennox), or were trying to pursue a policy of their own (like Hamilton), or were simply ignorant of the true situation there (like Laud). Military preparations were begun on both sides. The English army which was sent towards the Scottish border in the early summer of 1639 consisted largely of militia units plus volunteers — courtiers and professional soldiers of fortune. The Earl of Arundel was appointed commander-in-chief. His second in command was the third Earl of Essex, the son of Elizabeth's last favourite, who had been executed for an unsuccessful coup in 1601. The third Earl had been the victim of a notorious court scandal under James I, and had since served abroad as a professional soldier. Both armies depended much on officers and non-commissioned officers who had served on the Continent, often in the same armies — of the Dutch, German Protestants, and Swedes. In what came to be known later as the first of the 'Bishops' Wars' the two sides confronted each other across the river Tweed, but there was no real fighting. Peace was patched up, the armies drew back and the English forces largely melted away. The King made sweeping concessions which led to the enactment of a whole reform programme in the Scottish parliament and to the introduction of a more extreme form of presbyterianism in the church. It seems that Charles never regarded these concessions as more than tactical, a way of gaining time and dividing his opponents — a correct calculation, as it turned out, but on the wrong time scale, for this did not begin to take effect until 1641. Meanwhile at home more systematic preparations were started for a renewed English invasion, both by sea and land, scheduled for the summer of 1640.

Parliament Again

At least as important as these military plans, Charles decided to summon a new parliament on the advice of Wentworth, who was shortly to be created Earl of Strafford. Both King and minister seem to have been deceived by the relative ease with which Wentworth had manipulated the Irish parliament a few years earlier. The proportion of seats where elections were contested was probably higher than in any of the parliaments of the 1620s, but in the majority of constituencies members were still chosen by a process of patronage and negotiation. Only if family or party rivalries got out of hand was there resort to a poll or count of the voters. And this, of course, would have very different implications according to the type of seat, and whether it involved all the freeholders of a populous county, or a large town with something approaching male household suffrage, as against what would later come to be called a 'rotten borough' with only a handful of electors, or at most a few dozen, who were entitled to vote. But there seems little doubt that the elections and selections of MPs did reflect some of the discontents with royal policy over the whole period since the last parliament, notably Ship Money and what were seen as Laud's policies in the church.

The assembly which was formally opened on 13 April 1640 and was to be dissolved on 5 May has become known to history as the Short Parliament. It is easy to be wise after the event, but even at the time the King and his advisers were criticised for getting rid of this body so

precipitately. The main area of dispute was how much money in subsidies would the Commons vote in return for the King abandoning Ship Money and agreeing to an act against its ever being levied again except with parliamentary assent. Not surprisingly after eleven years, there were other grievances too. Some related to parliamentary privilege and the punishment of MPs and merchants after the 1629 session. Others arose from various aspects of royal revenue-raising measures, from the alleged misuse of the legal system, particularly through the prerogative courts, and from the régime of Laud and his allies in the church. It would be wrong to say for certain that Charles could have reached a mutually acceptable series of agreements with the Short Parliament; but, having summoned it at all, he should have persevered for longer, if only to try to put his critics in the wrong as he had contrived to do in 1629, although since the quality of the political leadership in the Commons was superior to what it had been then, this might not have worked.

Failure to reach an agreement, and notably to get any vote of immediate supply by the time of the dissolution, left very little room for manoeuvre. The King could have called off his military preparations and re-opened negotiations with the leading Covenanters, hoping to win over the more moderate among them by concessions, and otherwise letting time take its course in Scotland. Alternatively, he could continue to prepare for war, relying on non-parliamentary sources of supply and gambling on a quick victory.

The Second Bishops' War

Urged on by Strafford, Charles went for the second option. This time Northumberland was to be in command, perhaps because of his influence in the region, with Strafford as his deputy. This disgruntled Arundel and Essex who felt that displacement reflected on their honour; and this may help to explain the one's voluntary exile, the other's active leadership of the King's enemies in the Civil War. Through real or feigned ill health, Northumberland managed to take little part in the campaign which followed, and so to avoid being discredited; Strafford, though crippled by genuine illness, carried on heroically and took most of the blame. The vanguard of the two armies met some way inland from Berwick, on a small tributary of the Tweed; the English were disgracefully routed, and their whole army withdrew in a disorderly, unplanned retreat, leaving the Scots in occupation of the northernmost counties and threatening the borders of Yorkshire. The King's position was fatally undermined by this defeat. The double financial burden of Ship Money, together with the so-called 'Coat and Conduct' money payable when militia forces were moved outside their own counties, led to widespread non-payment, which has, with pardonable exaggeration, been called a 'taxpayers' strike'. Discipline in the English forces had already been poor when units on their way north had turned on officers who were, or were believed to be, Catholics; after the defeat at Newburn and loss of the north, many just straggled away, leaving the professionals who, like the Scots, needed to be paid. At the same time there was a sudden collapse of the Crown's creditworthiness; in modern terminology, Charles and his government faced an acute cash-flow problem.

Here the attitude of the City of London was crucial. So great a proportion of the liquid wealth of the country was concentrated there in so few hands that the response of a few dozen Londoners — the Lord Mayor and Aldermen, the senior members of the great trading and livery companies,

and a few freelance outsiders — could be decisive for the purposes of immediate borrowing. The state of Charles's relations with the élite of the City is therefore a matter of historical substance, and one on which the two leading modern authorities disagree. Some Londoners clearly disapproved of the Crown's policies in general, either for financial or religious reasons, but how many of the more influential felt this way and how strongly, is — as with opinion in the country generally before 1640 — a matter almost of informed guesswork. The City had specific grievances too. Whereas chartered trading companies had not come within the scope of the 1624 act against monopolies, the King had made grants to other groups of courtiers and business men which appeared to infringe these charters, notably in the case of the East India Company. Also the City had been sued in Star Chamber, allegedly for not having carried out its undertakings in the colonization of Ulster (as the present-day name of Londonderry still exists to remind us); a huge fine had been imposed, although the greater part was remitted. The Crown had incurred further odium by its attempted interference in the physical growth of London and the imposition of fines for wrongful suburban buildings and in-filling. The incorporation of the gilds and companies of Westminster, a kind of rival to the City of London, was another pointless affront. Popular Puritan preachers had been purged from some City churches. Rumours of the measures proposed to overcome the financial crisis in the summer of 1640 probably completed the process of alienation. So far, by contrast with 1626-7, the King and the Council had only tried to borrow from a limited circle — great officers of state and other royal officials and courtiers — and on the Queen's personal initiative from loyal Catholics in the country as a whole. And the amount thus raised was quite inadequate to the needs of the moment. So, when the King turned instead to the City, who had helped out on the security of Crown lands back in the later 1620s, and was met with a virtually complete refusal, this was indeed the last straw.

With his passion for precedent and formal correctness, Charles now resorted to another ancient constitutional precedent. He summoned all members of the peerage of England, lay and ecclesiastical, to meet him at York, in their capacity as the Great Council of the realm, not as the upper House of parliament. Quite what he expected to get out of this is not clear. In the face of a petition from twelve of them, including two future royalists, calling for a new parliament, he apparently decided to summon one without even waiting to consult the Great Council. This body spent much of its time discussing negotiations with the Scots, notably what concessions would be needed to get them out of the north of England. So the process of selection and election for the parliament which was to meet on 3 November, took place in the shadow of military defeat and financial crisis. This was most unfavourable to the King's and Court's interests, and was reflected in its membership.

The Long Parliament

The changes in the Commons since the spring were overwhelmingly towards the Country and away from the Court. Arguably, however, the change in the general temper of the membership was more important than that in its composition. Having fought and lost the Second Bishops' War since then, and now with two armies to be maintained — the Scots, as well as what was left of his own — the King's bargaining position was correspondingly much weakened. Whether our story should end here, with the meeting of parliament, in November 1640, or with the beginning of the Civil War nearly two years later, is a matter of judgment. The Personal Rule, in the sense of Charles's régime as it had operated hitherto, certainly collapsed with the opening of the Long Parliament. The subsequent breakdown of relations between King and Parliament, and the final resort to armed force resulting from that, was far from anyone's intentions at the end of 1640, even in the early part of 1641, and was due in part to developments not yet in view.

It may throw some further light on the state of things before 1640 if we review briefly the measures of the new parliament according to whether they seem to have been generally accepted, or to have helped create a reaction in the King's favour. To take these steps more or less in sequence: the Commons' pre-emptive blow to impeach Strafford was accepted by the Lords, who agreed to his imprisonment and the initial proceedings for his trial. Only as it dragged on inconclusively in the misconceived attempt to prove someone guilty of treason for having carried out the King's own policies with loyal efficiency, and the Commons majority's subsequent decision to proceed against him by attainder — a legislative rather than judicial method of removing someone — did the Lords hang back and have to be coerced by organized mass demonstrations of Londoners being used to threaten their safety. Likewise they accepted Laud's removal under threat of impeachment, though he was not brought to trial for another four years, and measures against other bishops, judges and monopolists; the two next most hated individual targets, Finch and Windebank, escaped overseas. Although the King had at first said that he would never accept it, the Act providing for a parliament to be called at least once every three years aroused little opposition; nor did measures against Ship Money and other financial devices of the 1630s, or those to ensure that the customs duties really were under parliamentary control; the prerogative courts of Star Chamber, and High Commission, and of the Council at York (which had been very much Strafford's instrument for breaking opposition in the north) had few defenders. The King may have been planning a counter-coup, to get rid of the parliament, as early as the spring of 1641, and this was used by the radical leaders in the two Houses to justify further measures to limit royal power, some of which began to generate a reaction in the King's favour. The two Acts passed almost simultaneously in May — for Strafford's attainder (and execution) and against the dissolution, or even temporary interruption, of the present parliament without its own consent — may well have marked the turning point. Few people seemed to have realised at the time how valuable a royal prerogative, tactically speaking, the King had abandoned in accepting the second of these, which was justified on grounds of financial necessity: that people would not go on lending to the Crown on the security of future revenues unless they had a guarantee that these would be legally collected with parliamentary consent. Even then, and in spite of further proposals to restrict the King's freedom of action, it seems to have been their attack on the Church which lost the parliamentarians most support. In order to obtain enough backing from the radical Puritans especially in London, for their own political programme, and to conciliate their Scottish allies, the radical leaders now went far beyond simply reversing the policies of Laud and the Arminians. Although several of them, including John Pym, had not started out from this position, they now committed themselves to the abolition of episcopacy followed, probably, by the replacement of the Prayer Book with something more like the form of worship used in Scotland and other churches under Genevan

influence. Meanwhile, the Scottish army had withdrawn from the north of England, sufficient money having been raised by the English parliament to persuade them to go home; likewise the King's remaining forces there had also been paid off. This had the effect of weakening the parliamentarians' bargaining position, since the King's need for regular supplies was no longer nearly so acute as before. Charles aimed to follow up this advantage by visiting Scotland and trying to win support there by bridging the gap between the old Court party and the less radical of the Covenanters, in which he achieved some limited success.

So we really have to explain two distinct, but closely related, developments between the summer of 1641 and the spring of 1642. Increasingly those with conservative instincts, whether on primarily religious or constitutional or social grounds, were now more alarmed by the Parliament than by the King, who recovered enough support, in England quite apart from Scotland, for a future royalist party to take shape. And, when civil war eventually came, the King was thus able to fight it on something like equal terms from 1642-5. Parallel to this, mutual suspicions of each other's intentions on the part of the parliamentary leaders and the King hardened to the point where normal relations broke down. And eventually both sides resorted to armed force in order to resist or coerce the other. On the Puritan-parliamentarian side, intensifying fear and suspicion focused on the alleged threat of a general Catholic conspiracy and the more real danger of a military coup, led by courtiers and demobilised army officers but acting under the King's inspiration if not with his direct knowledge. The credibility of this was immensely strengthened by two further developments: the outbreak of the Irish Rebellion in the autumn of

The Czech artist Wenceslaus Hollar (1606-77), whose patron was the Earl of Arundel, made many accurate drawings and etchings of buildings. This view shows New Palace Yard, one of the nerve-centres of public life, the open space in front of the parliament buildings and the law courts. Several of the courts sat in Westminster Hall, shown on the left here.

1641, and the affair of the Five Members at the beginning of January 1642. There were indeed Catholics both at home and abroad who still hoped to see Protestantism destroyed; just as the reverse was also true. Of a specific plot, however, there is very little evidence except in Ireland.

The unsuccessful attempt to seize the five MPs whom, together with one peer, the King had accused of treason, undid much of his gains from the time of Strafford's attainder to the Grand Remonstrance. This was a long catalogue of grievances presented to him in the autumn of 1641 and then published, in both cases, by hotly contested votes. In fact the margin of support for the Remonstrance was so narrow even in the Commons, and the possibility of its getting through the Lords so remote, that, if Charles and

his advisers had simply done nothing, support would have begun to ebb away from the opposition. Whether or not the King's coming into the House of Commons with his nephew, the Elector Palatine, leaving a large number of armed men in the lobby outside, was the gross breach of parliamentary privilege that was made out, it certainly suggested readiness on the King's part to use armed force against his opponents if he could get away with it. Since the five had been forewarned and were no longer in their places, and since the radical Puritans had just before this seized control of government in the City of London, which now provided a safe base for the parliamentarians, his failure left him worse off than before.

The Irish Rebellion

It was, however, the violent upheaval in Ireland which precipitated the final breach in England. Control of the militia had already been brought up as an issue earlier in 1641, but had not made much progress. The question now was who was to raise and to command the forces needed to crush the Irish and to repel possible foreign

31

1 You ar to accuse those [deleted] joinΘlie & severallie
2 you ar to reserue the power of making addicionally
3 When the Comitie for examinacion is a naming (wch yo^u
must presse to be close & under tey of secresie) if eather
Essex, Warwick, Holland, Say, [deleted] Wharton, o[r]
Brooke be named, you must desyre that they may be spared
because you ar to examine them as witnesses for me

The warrant for the arrest of the Five Members (together with one peer, Lord Mandeville, later Earl of Manchester), from the King to the Attorney-General. Only after the failure to get this order carried out did Charles I enter the House of Commons with his nephew, the Elector Palatine, leaving a large armed posse in the lobby outside. Looking round, and seeing none of the wanted Five, the King allegedly remarked, 'I see all the birds are flown', to cries of 'Privilege! Privilege!' from the assembled MPs.

Catholic invaders, Irish or others. Just as the Scottish resistance to the new Prayer Book of 1637, and all that had followed from this, had led to the end of Charles I's Personal Rule in England, so the rebellion in Ireland led to the outbreak of civil war a year later. The Personal Rule might have ended without the Scots, but certainly not as and when it did. There might have been a civil war in England in the 1640s but, without the Irish, not the one which did begin in 1642. So the downfall of Charles I had an Irish as well as a Scottish dimension.

It is ironical that the innovatory aspects of royal policy took longer to reveal themselves in Ireland than in either Scotland or England. Indeed, until the early 1630s, it is hard to say that Charles I had an Irish policy at all, except to maintain English rule more or less on the basis achieved under his father. James's last Deputy was continued in office until 1629; his recall and suspension saw a kind of interim government by Lords Justices. In practice this meant that power was in the hands of the so-called New English, the recent settlers. Whereas the Old English, as the Anglo-Irish were generally known, were in many cases of mixed descent, having intermarried with the Old Irish, or native inhabitants, and were also divided in religion, many having remained Catholic during the sixteenth-century Reformation, or even having reverted to Rome since then, the New English were both ethnically and denominationally a close-knit homogeneous group. They were strongly Protestant, mostly Calvinist in theology, but episcopalians except in Ulster, where the Scots who settled with James's active support in the 1610s were mainly presbyterian and constituted a fourth element in the population.

In 1632 Charles appointed his ablest and most vigorous minister, previously in charge of the north of England, as Lord Deputy. Thomas Wentworth, now a Viscount but already ambitious to become an Earl — an honour which he was not to attain until 1640 — only reached Dublin in the summer of 1633, but his presence was very quickly felt, not least by the New English clique previously in charge. It is not clear how far Charles I grasped the significance of his appointment. A man of unlimited ambition and very high ability, an idealist with a ruthless streak, Wentworth was determined to succeed where earlier viceroys had failed, both in imposing a coherent set of policies and in using his post there as a spring-board for returning to England at the appropriate time as undisputed chief minister and with wealth commensurate to this position. He was encouraged in almost all his purges and other reforms by his political ally and personal friend, Archbishop Laud. Indeed this was partly what they meant by 'Thorough' in their private correspondence. None the less, Wentworth was also dependent on the cooperation of other members of the government at home: the despised Portland and his ally Cottington, the worthy but uninspired Secretary Coke, Coventry on the legal side, and ultimately the King himself. In essence, personal and sectional vested interests, except those of the Lord Deputy himself and his own circle of friends and adherents, were to be totally subordinated to the aim of a financially solvent, militarily secure and economically prosperous country. Neither the New nor the Old English, nor the Ulster Scots, let alone the Old Irish must be allowed to stand in the way. To the extent that Ireland as a recently conquered and partially colonised territory formed a *tabula rasa*, in a way that neither England nor

Scotland could do, this ambition had a certain plausibility. In pursuit of his aims Wentworth was quite ready to use the Irish parliament, itself mainly representative of settler interests and thus less independent than its English counterpart. In this he was superficially very successful in 1634 and up to a point even as late as the spring of 1640.

To what extent Wentworth and Laud regarded Ireland as a kind of blue-print for 'Thorough' at home is not clear. By 1639-40 Strafford had made many enemies, and without the contents of his and Laud's letters being known, he was certainly regarded with alarm and suspicion. As we have seen, his misjudgment about the tractability of the English parliament was a strange mistake by someone who had himself been a leading MP in the 1620s. So it is not surprising that he and the Archbishop were, at one and the same time, the King's most efficient and dedicated servants, but also by 1640 two of his greatest liabilities on account of their extreme unpopularity. They were also two very convenient scapegoats, behind whom other members of the royal government were able to shelter when the storm broke.

Strafford was not the direct cause of the Irish Rebellion. He left the country for the last time in the spring of 1640 and was dead nearly six months before its outbreak. But his rule was its indirect cause. His immediate successor, Christopher Wandesford, a close friend and ally but with a much more amiable temperament, might have kept control of the situation, but himself died at the end of 1640. In a mistaken concession to the English opposition, Charles then reverted to rule by Lords Justices, which again meant the dominance of the New English. Fear of what a settler-dominated administration, pushed on by a Puritan parliament in England, might do to them and their faith, led sections of the Old Irish in Ulster and elsewhere to plan a rising, for which some of the organizers were to claim Charles's approval, one even having a forged commission from him. Whether anyone, for example in the Queen's circle, had given them encouragement is less clear but at least possible. For some, it was a last desperate attempt to recover the lands which they or their families had lost in the preceding generations; for others, something of a religious crusade, to save the Catholic faith, perhaps to regain the whole island for it. The plan went wrong. Dublin Castle was not captured, and in the north at first, but spreading from there to other areas, ghastly, unplanned atrocities began on both sides. Out of this developed a bloody, if intermittent, eleven-year-long conflict: an unsuccessful rebellion, or an abortive war of liberation, depending on your viewpoint.

This is not our story here. Out of this situation arose the final confrontation in England during the early part of 1642. The King eventually, to his shame as it may be thought, agreed to pledge the lands of Irish not yet convicted of rebellion, as the financial security for the soldiers, munitions and ships which would be needed in the reconquest. But he would not give way over control of the armed forces at home. His rejection of Parliament's Militia bill led to their proceeding by way of ordinance, legislation by the two Houses of Parliament without the royal assent. This logical, but legally revolutionary, step led almost immediately to military preparations by both sides, although a long propaganda campaign preceded the outbreak of fighting. Each party was very keen to put the other in the wrong, especially as there was widespread feeling in the country against civil war and many attempts by individuals, and by the gentry of whole counties, to keep out and remain neutral. The King and his supporters claimed to be putting down a rebellion; the parliamentarians to be fighting to defend their religion, liberty and property. In the summer and early autumn of 1642, as military operations commenced, no one could foresee the outcome. Here we are right to stop, and forgo the wisdom of hindsight.

Long-term Changes?

Were there any underlying aspects of English life at this time which may help to explain the short-term successes and failures of royal government? The so-called Price Revolution, or gradual inflation, which had begun in the early sixteenth century, was nearing its end. Disregarding short-run fluctuations in grain prices due to good and bad harvests, and trade booms and slumps due to conditions in the country's export markets, prices became more stable by the mid- seventeenth century, and there was to be no massive, sustained increase again until the later eighteenth century. Likewise population growth, which had been relatively rapid over the whole span from the early sixteenth century, had perhaps been at its fastest from about 1560 to about 1620, and was to flatten out for almost a century from around 1640. Closely related to these fundamental features, the market in landed property was probably at its most active in the very early seventeenth century; indeed, one leading historian has suggested that it was never to be more active again until the end of the nineteenth and beginning of the twentieth century. The growth of higher education, too, measured by the numbers of students entering the two universities and the Inns of Court (for training in the common law), may also have peaked in the 1620s and 1630s. In a society where most landed property passed to eldest sons, and where the opportunities for advancement in business and the professions were strictly limited, this may have created a pressure for upward social mobility which the economy and the structure of society were unable to satisfy. The church was the most ancient and prestigious of the learned professions, but it offered poor financial rewards and, for reasons already suggested, had become ideologically unattractive to many potential entrants. The law was easily the most buoyant profession, but hard to get into, still harder to rise in, without family connections or other patronage; and the rewards within the legal profession were very unevenly distributed. Medicine was a much smaller, though fast-growing, profession, but only the physicians were regarded as intellectually and socially respectable; the surgeons and apothecaries, however skilful and effective, enjoyed an inferior status. Likewise in the world of commerce, a gentleman's son could be apprenticed to a London merchant or to a financier, but not to a manufacturer or retailer without serious loss of status.

Put crudely and with numerous exceptions, the economic and demographic changes of the previous century or so had made the rich richer and the poor poorer. Moreover, some taxes of the 1630s, such as Ship Money, reached further down, to affect less affluent levels in the community than the traditional subsidies had done. Few historians would deny that the wage-earning section of society was worse off in real terms than it had been at the end of the fifteenth century. But, correspondingly, very few historians would today speak in terms of a rising bourgeoisie, that is of a business middle-class rising at the expense of the landed aristocracy. The Crown, the Church and the labouring classes were worse off, poorer in real terms; most of the upper and middle ranks of society were better off than they ever had been before. Moreover, few historians would still take the view

that particular ranks or sections within these classes were rising or declining: there is not enough evidence that gentry were doing better than peers, or that medium-sized landowners were better able to prosper than those with great estates; conversely, there is even less evidence that 'mere' gentry without court, mercantile or professional connections were unable to make ends meet. On the other hand, in spite of being doubled in size by royal creations between 1603 and 1630, the lay peerage was still a very small group, from which younger sons dropped out unless they subsequently inherited from childless elder brothers or were themselves ennobled (like Montgomery and Holland). By contrast, the gentry class was much more open at the bottom, to entry either by younger sons of existing gentry families, or by successful yeomen and tenant farmers, merchants and members of the professions. To the extent that it was, in this way, a growing social group, the gentry was perhaps, in truth, increasing its total share of the national wealth; but this is not really what was meant by R.H. Tawney's famous phrase 'the rise of the gentry'. The attempts of various historians to correlate 'new', rising or entrepreneurially successful gentry with the religious and political opposition to the early Stuarts have all foundered; so too with the reverse of this. The only social or economic distinctions which still appear to be accepted are that, within the landed classes, future royalists were on average younger than future parliamentarians, and that future royalists were likely to be more heavily in debt; but borrowing could as easily have been a symptom of economic buoyancy as of a spendthrift attitude, although heavy gambling with its unhappy consequences was more a feature of the Court than of the Puritan counter-culture.

The fact that agricultural prices were

A view of Greenwich, painted for Charles I in 1632 by Adrian van Stalbent, a Flemish landscape artist, and Jan van Belcamp. The Tudor palace can be seen, also the half-completed Queen's House, a more modest-sized Italianate villa, designed by Inigo Jones. It was begun in 1616 for James I's queen, Anne of Denmark (Charles I's mother). Work was halted on her death and only started again in 1630, for Queen Henrietta Maria. She is seen in the foreground, next to the King and the young Prince Charles, with courtiers and attendants, including the Earl of Portland (in black) and Endymion Porter, Groom of the Bedchamber and a personal favourite of the King (on the left).

rising faster than either wages or the costs of manufactures, suggests that population was growing faster than output. Yet new methods of land use and techniques of husbandry were certainly spreading, and more land was being brought under cultivation with the reclamation of fens, forests and common wastes; in consequence total agricultural output was rising. By the third quarter of the seventeenth century, improvements leading to increased productivity were to produce a swing the other way, with a down-turn in farm prices, and a fall in rents.

England's foreign trade was in a process of re-alignment. Diversification was taking place, away from excessive dependence on the export of heavyweight woollens to northern and central Europe. Again by the later seventeenth century, a big shift was under way, to a wider range of foreign markets; there was also a remarkable growth in the importation and then the re-export of colonial and other overseas products to continental Europe. And English merchant shipping was beginning to win a larger share of the carrying trade of the western world as a whole, from its Dutch competitors. The changes in methods of finance were to be more striking than those in industrial production until well into the next century. A new, and vastly superior, system of government credit and borrowing was to emerge, though this was still far away in the 1630s; but at least the Crown did not tamper seriously with the currency.

There was another new development, beginning in the seventeenth century. After a false start under Elizabeth, English colonization in North America had begun in the reign of James. But more English (as well as Scots) went to settle in Ireland at that time than crossed the Atlantic. Emigration to America quickened in the 1620s, with the rise of the Virginia tobacco trade and the earliest English use of Black African slave labour. From 1629 to 1640 there was a much larger exodus, to New England, Virginia and the Caribbean Islands. How far the emigrants' motives were religious or political, like those of refugees in modern times, has been much disputed among historians for a long time; and the evidence available permits of no certain answer. However, we can say that, even if the majority of people went for primarily material, rather than ideological reasons, in order — as they hoped — to better their conditions, emigration must also have acted as a kind of 'safety valve' inside England, lowering social, and so indirectly,

political tensions. Evidence for a strong ideological element, at least among a minority of those going to New England, is shown in the growing hostility between the Massachusetts Bay Company and the royal government by the late 1630s. If Charles I and his Council had not been beset by worse troubles nearer home, they might well have sent an expeditionary force across the North Atlantic, to bring Massachusetts and the other New England settlements to heel, 130 years before the skirmishes at Lexington and Concord which were to help precipitate the American Declaration of Independence.

In the mental world of the time, there is some evidence that scepticism was growing with regard to accusations of witchcraft. In this respect Charles I was less credulous than his father had been. Resort to astrologers, faith healers and amateur psychiatrists or counsellors ('white witches' as both these categories were known) was widespread at every social level. At the same time there are indications of new attitudes, and of growing interest in scientific advances, notably in mathematics, astronomy, mechanics and medicine, in which the King himself seems to have shared.

It is possible to argue that none of the processes of adjustment and modernization discussed in the preceding paragraphs would have come to fruition without the revolutionary upheavals of the 1640s and 1650s, or something like them. This, I think, would still be Christopher Hill's fundamental interpretation of the period. And we should certainly be very cautious about arguing the contrary proposition: namely that the country's problems were all in the process of solving themselves and might have done so even more successfully and speedily without the hurtful influence of political and religious conflicts. Although people in

The Royal BANQUETING HOUSE in Whitehal

the 1630s could not have known this, it does look as if on balance the longer-term influences at work were favourable to stability rather than the reverse. In that sense they would have been likely to make the country more, not less, governable. For this reason, and because the régime's control over the educational system would be likely to influence the outlook of the rising generation, time should have been on the side of the King and his administration, and against those who were most unhappy with the tendencies in church and state which his régime represented.

Conclusion: a general view

There are other, even less tangible, questions which we might ask. How far was King Charles personally responsible for what went on in the country, both for better and for worse? Was England a happy, prosperous, contented country in the years before the Civil War? The former raises the whole issue of free will and determinism and the role of the individual in history. Short of believing that history is predetermined by impersonal forces beyond the capacity

The Banqueting House, in Whitehall, London, was begun in 1619. Its innovatory design by Inigo Jones was influenced by his study of buildings by the Italian Renaissance architect Palladio. King Charles commissioned Rubens to paint the allegorical subjects which adorn the interior ceiling panels with such exuberance. They include the Apotheosis of James I with Justice, Zeal, Religion, Honour, and Victory; the King pointing to Peace and Plenty embracing; and Minerva driving Rebellion to Hell. Ironically it was through one of the windows of this room that King Charles stepped out to place his head on the executioner's block, on 30 January 1649.

---

of any individual to influence, then in a system of personal, hereditary monarchy, the king or queen reigning at the time must count for a great deal, in their choice of subordinates — ministers, favourites and others — as well as in the pursuit of particular policies. With regard to the condition of England, over a timespan of half a generation or less[***] the historian can as it were try to take the temperature, but it is scarcely possible to measure economic growth, social change or cultural wellbeing. The 1630s were not a 'golden age'. Yet it is entirely comprehensible that royalists and anglicans should have looked back to it as such, especially during the years of their defeat in the 1640s and 1650s. And the country was at peace while large parts of the continent were being ravaged by a bloody, and seemingly endless, war.

If we are to apportion responsibility, then the King tragically, because he was a fallible and limited but not an evil man, was his own worst enemy. Charles I did more to bring about the downfall of his system than any other single influence, let alone any other individual.

*** *Reckoning that the average eldest son in the upper classes married at about twenty five and had his first child a year or so later.*

Bibliography: 2nd Edition

With one exception, I have not offered critical opinions about present-day historians in this booklet. It would, however, be cowardly, and unhelpful to the reader to say nothing about any of these additions. Russell (No. 7) is the subtlest and most profound analysis, although Hughes (no. 5) provides an interpretation with which I am most in agreement myself. While in my view Sharpe (no. 9) tends to give Charles I and his advisers the benefit of the doubt too often and too much, this is now the best as well as the fullest account of the Personal Rule written in this century: the fruit of ten years' research and a major achievement of historical scholarship.

Note:
1. Place of publication is London unless given otherwise.
2. * indicates a text-book or general survey, with bibliography.

(1) Andrews, K.R., *Ships, Money and Politics: seafaring and naval enterprise in the reign of Charles I* (Cambridge, 1991).

(2) Cust, R. and Hughes, A. (eds.), *Conflict in early Stuart England: studies in religion and politics 1603-1642* (London, 1989).

(3) Davies, Julian, *The Caroline Captivity of the Church. Charles I and the Remoulding of Anglicanism 1625-1641* (Oxford, 1992).

(4) Fowler, Alastair (ed.), *The New Oxford Book of Seventeenth-Century Verse* (Oxford, 1991).

(5) Hughes, Ann, *The Causes of the English Civil War* (Basingstoke and London, 1991).

(6) Reeve, L.J., *Charles I and the road to Personal Rule* (Cambridge, 1989).

(7) Russell, C., *The Causes of the English Civil War: the Ford lectures delivered in the university of Oxford, 1987-1988* (Oxford, 1990).

(8) Russell, C., *The Fall of the British Monarchies 1637-1642* (Oxford, 1991).

(9) Sharpe, Kevin, *The Personal Rule of Charles I* (New Haven and London, 1992).

(10) Ashton, R., *The Crown and the Money Market 1603-42* (Oxford, 1960).

(11) Ashton, R., *The City and the Court 1603-43* (Cambridge, 1979).

(12) Aston, T.H., (ed.) *Crisis in Europe, 1560-1660* (1965 and later reprints).

(13) Aylmer, G.E., *The King' Servants ... 1625-1642* (1961: rev. edn., 1974).

(14) Barnes, T.G., *Somerset 1625-1640: A County's Government under the Personal Rule* (1961).

(15) Boynton, L.O., *The Elizabethan Militia 1558-1638* (1967).

(16) Brunton, D. and Pennington, D.H., *Members of the Long Parliament* (1954: repr. Hamden, Conn., 1968).

* (17) Bush, D., *English Literature in the Earlier 17th Century* (rev. edn. Oxford, 1962).

(18) Butler, M., *Theatre in Crisis 1632-1642* (Cambridge, 1984).

* (19) Canny, N., *From Reformation to Restoration: Ireland 1534-1660* (Dublin, 1987).

(20) Clarendon, Edward Hyde earl of, *The History of the Rebellion ...* ed. W.D. Macray (6 vols. Oxford, 1888, but in print).

(21) Clark, P., *English Provincial Society ... 1500-1640*, on Kent (Hassocks, Suss., 1977).

(22) Clark, P., and Slack, P.A., (eds.), *Crisis and Order in English Towns 1500-1700* (1972).

* (23) **Clark, P., and Slack, P.A.**, (eds.), *English Towns in Transition 1500-1700* (Oxford, 1976).
* (24) **Clay, C.G.A.**, *Economic Expansion and Social change: England 1500-1700* (2 vols. Cambridge, 1984).
(25) **Cliffe, J.T.**, *The Yorkshire Gentry From the Reformation to the Civil War* (1969).
(26) **Cliffe, J.T.**, *The Puritan Gentry* (1984).
(27) **Cooper J.P.**, *Land, Men and Beliefs* (1983).
(28) **Cooper J.P.**, (ed.) *New Cambridge Modern History*, IV, *1609-1648/59* (Cambridge, 1970), ch.xix, 'The Fall of the Stuart Monarchy'.
(29) **Cope, E.S.**, *Politics without Parliaments 1629-1640* (1987).
* (30) **Coward, B.**, *The Stuart Age 1603-1714* (1980).
(31) **Cust, R.**, *The Forced Loan in English Politics 1626-8* (Oxford, 1987).
(32) *Dictionary of National Biography.*
(33) **Dietz, F.C.**, *English Public Finance 1558-1641* (N.Y. 1932; repr. London, 1964).
(34) **Donaldson, G.**, *The Making of the Scottish Prayer Book of 1637* (Edinburgh, 1954).
(35) **Fisher, F.J.**, (ed.) *Essays in the Economic and Social History of Tudor and Stuart England: Presented to R.H. Tawney* (Cambridge, 1961).
(36) **Fletcher, A.J.**, *A County Community in Peace and War: Sussex 1600-1660* (1976).
(37) **Fletcher, A.J.**, *The Outbreak of the English Civil War* (1981).
(38) **Fletcher, A.J.**, *Reform in the Provinces: the Government of Stuart England* (New Haven and London, 1986).
(39) **Gardiner, S.R.**, *History of England . . . 1603-1642* (rev. edn. 10 vols. 1883-4; repr. 1980s).
(40) **Gardiner, S.R.**, (ed.) *Constitutional Documents of the Puritan Revolution 1625-1660* (repr. Oxford, 1980).
(41) **Haller, W.**, *The Rise of Puritanism 1570-1643* (N.Y. 1938 and 1957: paperb. Philadelphia, 1972), (later chs.).
(42) **Haller, W.**, *Liberty and Reformation in the Puritan Revolution* (N.Y. 1955) (earlier chs.).
(43) **Hexter, J.H.**, *The Reign of King Pym* (Cambridge, Mass, 1941).
(44) **Hexter, J.H.**, *Re-Appraisals in History* (1961).
(45) **Hibberd, C.**, *Charles I and the Popish Plot* (Chapel Hill, N. Ca., 1983).
(46) **Hill, C.**, *Economic Problems of the Church from Archbishop Whitgift to the Long Parliament* (Oxford, 1956), Pt. III.
(47) **Hill, C.**, *Society and Puritanism*

in *Pre-Revolutionary England* (1964).

* (48) Hill, C., *The Century of Revolution 1603-1714* (Edinburgh, 1961; rev. edn. Walton-on-Thames, 1980).

(49) Hill, C., *Intellectual Origins of the English Revolution* (Oxford, 1965).

(50) Hill, C. and Dell, E., (eds.), *The Good Old Cause* (1949: repr. 1969), Pts. One to Six.

(51) Hirst, D., *The Representative of the People? Voters and Voting in England under the Early Stuarts* (Cambridge, 1975).

* (52) Hirst D., *Authority and Conflict England 1603-58* (1986).

(53) Holmes, C., *Seventeenth-Century Lincolnshire* (Lincoln, 1980).

(54) Howell, R., *Newcastle-upon-Tyne and the Puritan Revolution* (Oxford, 1967).

(55) Hughes, A., *Politics, Society and Civil War in Warwickshire 1620-1660* (Cambridge, 1987).

(56) Hunt, W., *The Puritan Moment: The Coming of Revolution in an English County*, on Essex (Cambridge, Mass, 1983).

(57) James, M.E., *Family, Lineage and Civil Society . . . The Durham Region 1500-1640* (Oxford, 1974).

(58) Jones, W.J., *Politics and the Bench: The Judges and the Origins of the English Civil War* (1971).

(59) Judson, M.A., *The Crisis of the Constitution . . . 1603-1645* (New Brunswick, N.J., 1949, repr. N.Y. 1964).

(60) Kearney, H., *Strafford in Ireland* (Manchester, 1958).

* (61) Kenyon, J.P., (ed.), *The Stuart Constitution 1603-88* (Cambridge, 1966: rev. edn. 1986).

(62) Kishlansky, M.A., *Parliamentary Selection: social and political choice in early modern England* (Cambridge, 1986).

(63) Lamont, W.M., *Godly Rule . . . 1603-60* (1969).

(64) Lee, M., Jr., *The Road to Revolution: Scotland under Charles I, 1625-37* (Urbana and Chicago, 1985).

(65) Levack, B.P., *The Civil Lawyers in England 1603-42: A Political Study* (Oxford, 1973).

(66) Lloyd-Jones, H., Pearl, V., and Worden, A.B. (eds.), *History and Imagination: Essays in Honour of H.R. Trevor-Roper* (1981).

(67) Lockyer, R., *Buckingham: The Life and Political Career of George Villiers, First Duke of Buckingham 1592-1628* (1981).

(68) Manning, B.S. (ed.), *Politics, Religion and the English Civil War* (1973).

(69) Manning, B.S., *The English People and the English Revolution* (1976), earlier chs.

* (70) Millar, O. and Whinney, M., *The Oxford History of English Art 1625-*

1714 (Oxford, 1957).

* (71) Mitchison, R., *Lordship to Patronage: Scotland 1603-1745* (1983).

* (72) Moody, T.W. et al., *A New History of Ireland,* III, *1534-1692* (Oxford, 1976), chs. VIII-X.

(73) Morrill, J.S., *The Revolt of the Provinces 1630-1650* (1976: rev. edn. 1980).

(74) Morrill, J.S., *Cheshire 1630-1660* (Oxford, 1974).

(75) Ollard, R. and Tudor-Craig, P., (eds.), *For Veronica Wedgwood These: Studies in Seventeenth-century History* (1986).

(76) Pearl, V., *London and the Outbreak of the Puritan Revolution 1625-1643* (Oxford, 1961).

(77) Pennington, D.H. and Thomas, K., (eds.), *Puritans and Revolutionaries: Essays presented to Christopher Hill* (Oxford, 1978: paperb. 1982).

(78) Pocock, J.G.A., *The Ancient Constitution and the Feudal Law. A Study of English Historical Thought in the 17th Century* (Cambridge, 1957: 2nd edn. with 'A Retrospect', 1987).

(79) Prest, W., *The Inns of Court under Elizabeth I and the Early Stuarts 1590-1640* (Oxford, 1972).

(80) Prest, W., *The Rise of the Barristers: A Social History of the English Bar 1590-1640* (Oxford, 1986).

* (81) Richardson, R.C., *The Debate on the English Revolution* (1977).

(82) Russell, C., (ed.) *The Origins of the English Civil War* (1973).

(83) Russell, C., *Parliaments and English Politics 1621-9* (Oxford, 1979).

(84) Seaver, P., *The Puritan Lectureships* (Stanford, Cal., 1970).

(85) Seaver, P., *Wallington's World: A Puritan Artisan in 17th-century London* (1985).

(86) Slack, P.A., *The Impact of Plague in Tudor and Stuart England* (1985).

* (87) Slack, P.A., *Poverty and Policy in Tudor and Stuart England* (1988).

* (88) Sharpe, J.A., *Crime in Early-Modern England 1550-1750* (1984).

* (89) Sharpe, J.A., *Early Modern England: a social history 1550-1760* (1987).

(90) Sharpe, K.M., (ed.) *Faction and Parliament: Essays on Early Stuart History* (Oxford, 1978; paperb. L. 1985).

(91) Sharpe, K.M., *Criticism and Compliment: The Politics of Literature in the England of Charles I* (Cambridge, 1987).

(92) Simon, J., *Education and Society in Tudor England* (Cambridge, 1966), comes down to 1640.

* (93) Smith, A.G.R., *The Emergence of a Nation State, 1529-1660* (1984).

* (94) Smout, T.C., *History of the Scottish People,* I, *1560-1830* (1969), chs. II-VIII.

(95) Smuts, M., *Court Culture and the Origins of a Royalist Tradition in Early Stuart England* (Philadelphia, 1987).

(96) Sommerville, J.P., *Politics and Ideology in England 1603-1640* (1986).

(97) Starkey, D. *et al. The English Court: from the Wars of the Roses to the Civil War* (1987).

(98) Stevenson, D., *The Scottish Revolution 1637-44: The Triumph of the Covenanters* (Newton Abbot, 1973).

(99) Stone, L., *The Crisis of the Aristocracy 1558-1641* (Oxford, 1965).

(100) Stone, L., *Social Change and Revolution 1540-1640* (1965).

(101) Stone, L., *The Causes of the English Revolution 1529-1642* (1972 and reprs.).

(102) Supple, B., *Commercial Crisis and Change in England 1600-42* (Cambridge, 1959).

* (103) Thirsk, J., (ed.) *The Agrarian History of England and Wales,* IV, *1500-1640* (Cambridge, 1967).

(104) Thirsk, J., *Economic Policy and Projects* (Oxford, 1978: paperb. 1988).

(105) Thirsk, J. and Cooper, J.P., (eds.), *17th-Century Economic Documents* (Oxford, 1970).

(106) Thomas, K., *Religion and the Decline of Magic* (1971: paperb. 1973 in print).

(107) Thomas, K., *Man and the Natural World* (1983: paperb. Harmondsworth, 1984).

(108) Tomlinson, H., (ed.), *Before the Civil War* (1983).

(109) Trevor-Roper, H.R., *Life of Archbishop Laud 1573-1645* (1940; 2nd edn. 1962; 3rd edn. 1988/9).

(110) Trevor-Roper, H.R., *Catholics, Anglicans and Puritans: 17th-Century Essays* (1987).

(111) Tyacke, N., *Anti-Calvinists: the rise of English Arminianism c. 1590-1640* (Oxford, 1987).

(112) Underdown, D., *Revel, Riot and Rebellion: Popular Politics and Culture in England 1603-1660* (Oxford, 1986).

(113) Webster, C., *The Great Instauration, Science, Medicine and Reform 1626-1660* (1975).

(114) Wedgwood, C.V., *The King's Peace 1637-1641* (1955).

(115) Wedgwood, C.V., *Thomas Wentworth, First Earl of Strafford: a revaluation* (1961).

(116) Williams, Glanmor, *Recovery, Reorientation and Reformation: Wales c. 1415-1642* (Oxford, 1987).

* (117) Wrightson, K., *English Society 1580-1680* (1982).

(118) Zagorin, P., *The Court and the Country: The Beginning of the English Revolution* (1969).